HEATHCLIFF FEAST

by

ace books

A Division of Charter Communications Inc.
A GROSSET & DUNLAP COMPANY
51 Madison Avenue
New York, New York 10010

 # 1

...SYNDICATED CAT COMIC IN THE UNITED STATES AND OVERSEAS !

...IN MANY POLLS OF MAJOR NEWSPAPERS !

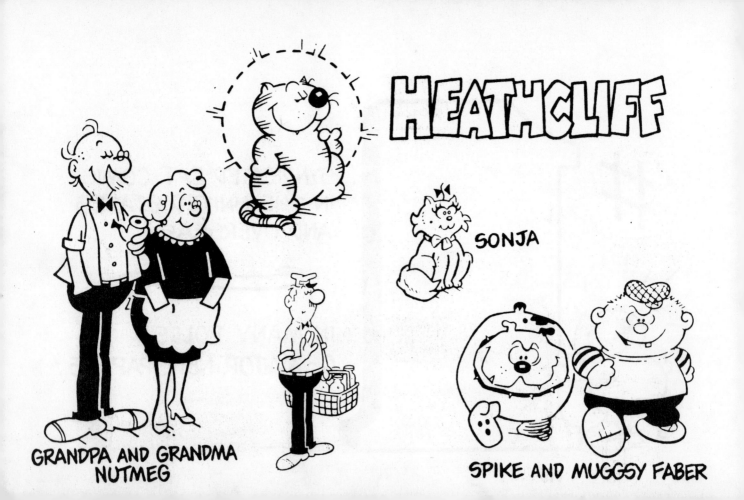

HEATHCLIFF

GRANDPA AND GRANDMA
NUTMEG

SONJA

SPIKE AND MUGGSY FABER

"HE'S IN GREAT SHAPE, BUT **I** NEED A DOCTOR!"

"TIMB.................ER!"

"BATTLE STATIONS!!"

"FANCY MEETING YOU HERE!"

"WELL, HOW WOULD **YOU** LIKE TO BE SAT ON?"

"I DON'T KNOW...I THINK IT'S A TOSS-UP WHICH ONE IS WORSE."

"THAT'S THE THIRD TIME THIS WEEK THAT CAT HAS DISRUPTED OUR CLASSROOM!"

"IT'S HIS HOT LINE TO THE DAIRY FARM."

"OH-OH...."

"HE BROKE UP THE BRIDGE CLUB AGAIN."

"NOW PROMISE MAMA YOU WON'T DO TO *THIS* MAN WHAT YOU DID TO THE *LAST* ONE."

"THAT'S WHAT YOU GET FOR RIFLING
THE BRANDIED PEACHES."

"THERE YOU GO, PLAYING FAVORITES AGAIN!"

"SIX SLIPPERS AND THREE BOOTS...
HE MUST HAVE MADE QUITE A RACKET
LAST NIGHT!"

"LOOK INTO MY EYES..."

"MEOW.... MEOW.... MEOW...."

"I WONDER IF HEATHCLIFF HAS NOTICED OUR NEW NEIGHBOR'S FEMALE CAT YET?"

"JUST DROP THEM IN HIS MOUTH...
IT'S HIS BIRTHDAY."

"NO, BUT I'LL KEEP AN EYE OPEN."

"THAT WILL BE $18.50 FOR YOUR SWEATER AND $16.98 FOR *HIS*!"

"WELL, SO MUCH FOR OUR NEIGHBOR'S NEW WATCH-DOG."

"TWO BANANA SPLITS...ONE WITH WALNUTS AND ONE WITH ANCHOVIES."

"I CAN'T UNDERSTAND IT... BESSIE HARDLY GAVE ANY MILK TODAY."

"WHAT MADE YOU THINK HIS BITE NEEDED CORRECTING ?!"

"SUP........PER!"

"NEXT TIME, GET HIS NAILS CLIPPED!"

"HEATHCLIFF!"

"GRANDMA, WAIT'LL I SHOW YOU WHAT HEATHCLIFF BROUGHT HOME, ONCE IT STOPS WRIGGLING."

"THERE'S A SIGHT YOU DON'T SEE VERY OFTEN."

"ABOUT THAT FROZEN PIZZA.."

"ARE THEY ALL FLYING SOUTH FOR THE WINTER, GRANDPA?"

"NOT WILLINGLY."

"GET IN THERE, HEATHCLIFF
AND BITE THE FULLBACK!"

"I THOUGHT I LEFT
YOU HOME!"

"IT'S THAT PESTY CAT AGAIN!"

"THERE ARE A LOT OF CAT FIGHTS IN THIS NEIGHBORHOOD... MOSTLY BETWEEN ME AND HEATHCLIFF!"

"HERE COMES THE PUNCH, FOLKS!"

"I THINK HE'S BEEN HITTING THE CATNIP AGAIN."

"DUE TO CIRCUMSTANCES BEYOND OUR CONTROL..."

"THEN AGAIN, IN SOME WAYS, THEY'RE VERY MUCH ALIKE."

"HELP!"

"NOW, HOW DID HE GET OUT OF
HIS CARRIAGE?"

"WE'RE DOWN HERE, GRANDMA...
ENTERTAINING MRS. FINCHLEY."

"WE THINK HEATHCLIFF IS PART PERSIAN
AND PART SIAMESE."

"I'D SAY PART TIGER AND PART ALLEY."

"HEATHCLIFF CAUGHT *THAT* ONE."

"HEATHCLIFF NEVER COULD RESIST TWEED."

"HEAVY DATE TONIGHT?"

"HOW ABOUT...

...THAT!"

"WHATEVER YOU DO, DON'T BRING UP
THE SUBJECT OF CATS."

"I TRIED PUTTING HEATHCLIFF
ON A DIET TODAY."

"...AND IT'S A VERY PEACEFUL NEIGHBORHOOD...

...WITH *ONE* EXCEPTION..."

"THE SITTER LEFT SHORTLY AFTER YOU DID."

"I CAN'T UNDERSTAND IT... I'VE BEEN DRUMMED OUT OF THE SOCIETY OF BIRD WATCHERS!"

"NEVER MIND THE DISGUISE!...
I KNOW IT'S YOU!!"

"AND NOW BACK TO OUR MOVIE ...
'CURSE OF THE CAT PEOPLE'..."

"COME ON, FOLKS...DINNER'S ON THE TABLE."

"HELP!"

"HE ATE MY STETHOSCOPE!"

"HEATHCLIFF COLLECTS THEM."

"FOUR AND TWENTY BLACKBIRDS, BAKED IN A PIE..."

"HE SINGS HERE EVERY NIGHT."

"HOW MANY TIMES MUST I TELL YOU, THEY'RE NOT MOUSE HOLES!"

SWAT!

"OH, HE DOESN'T READ THEM...HE CHEWS THEM."

"I'M WARNING YOU FOR THE LAST TIME...SCAT!"

"HE CERTAINLY HAS MADE A NAME
FOR HIMSELF IN THIS TOWN."

"HE DOES THAT EVERYTIME THE PRICE
GOES UP!"

"OH, HELLO, MACTAVISH....HMMMM?...
HEATHCLIFF STOLE *WHAT* FROM YOUR SCOTTY?"

"HE KNOWS VERY WELL WHAT HAT!"

"OH, LOOK, DEAR!... A HARBINGER OF...

...SPRING."

"FOR SOME UNKNOWN REASON, HE TOOK A DISLIKE TO THE CIRCUS STRONG MAN."

"THIS CAR IS GETTING A TERRIBLE SQUEAK IN IT!"

PLUNK

"WAIT 'TILL YOU SEE HARRY'S COSTUME FOR THE PARTY!...HARRY?"

"I TELL YOU SOMETHING JUST PEEKED IN THAT WINDOW!!"

"WE'LL USE HEATHCLIFF'S BLANKET AS A TABLECLOTH."

"CROSS OFF ANOTHER PROSPECTIVE CUSTOMER."

"COOKIE?"

"WHAT COULD I DO?...HE'S GOT THE FIVE BUCKS!"

"AND HOW WAS THE FLOUNDER, MADAM?"

"WHO IS THIS 'HEATHCLIFF' YOU KEEP REFERRING TO AS THE MAJOR CAUSE OF YOUR PROFIT LOSS?"

"NOW, LET'S PUT IT ON THE WINDOW-SILL TO COOL."

"I GUESS HE NEVER SAW A DACHSHUND BEFORE."

FLEA CIRCUS

4-18

"DID YOU PUT HEATHCLIFF OUT FOR THE NIGHT?"

"ABOUT THIS NEW BRAND OF CAT FOOD
YOU BOYS CAME UP WITH..."

"IT'S THE ONLY WAY I CAN GET HEATHCLIFF
TO TAKE HIS VITAMINS."

"I CAN'T PRACTICE WITH YOU SINGING!"

"I THINK HE'S CHECKING YOUR CREDENTIALS."

"I'LL WATCH MY *OWN* WEIGHT, THANK YOU!"

"NEVER WEAR THAT HAT AROUND HEATHCLIFF!"

"VISITING HOURS ARE OVER!"

"I WANT YOU TO GET BUSY AND CLEAN
YOUR GOLD-FISH BOWL."

"HEATHCLIFF LOVES TO SHAKE UP COLONEL BOOMER."

"HE'S HAVING ONE OF THOSE DAYS."

"YOU'RE LUCKY IT STOPPED RAINING."

"TOO MUCH HOWLING LAST NIGHT"

"DO WE ACCEPT CREDIT CARDS FROM CATS?"

"WHAT DO YOU MEAN, YOU CAN'T FIND MY TEETH?!"

"ER, PROFESSOR... ABOUT YOUR EXPERIMENT
WITH THE WHITE MICE AND THE BELL..."

"HEATHCLIFF!"

"HEATHCLIFF, I WISH YOU'D BE MORE CAREFUL WITH YOUR RUBBER MOUSE!"

"LOOK! I CAN HANDLE THIS!!"

"WATCH THIS, FRED... HEATHCLIFF CAN OPEN OUR NEW DOOR ALL BY HIMSELF!"

"SCAT!!"

"HE THINKS IT'S A SCRATCHING POST."

"HEATHCLIFF LOVES TO SEE SOMEONE *ELSE* BEING PUT OUT FOR THE NIGHT."

"I DON'T THINK HEATHCLIFF
LIKES HIS NEW COLLAR."

7-17

"HEATHCLIFF IS IN THE MIDST OF ANOTHER TRIANGLE."

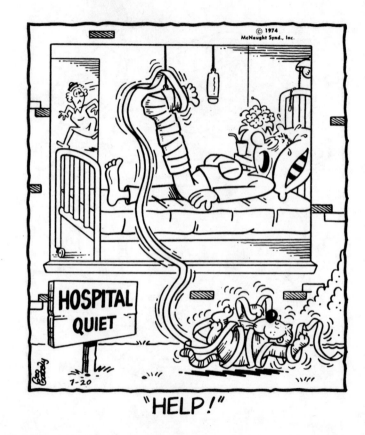

HOSPITAL
QUIET

7-20

"HELP!"

"*WOW!*... IT MUST BE A WHOPPER, GRAMPS!"

"HAS HE GONE?!"

"IT'S WHAT'S LEFT OF THE SCRATCHING POST YOU SOLD US FOR HEATHCLIFF."

"I KEEP HEARING SNICKERING!"

"THIS IS THE FIRST TIME WE'VE EVER BEEN CALLED TO GET A FIREMAN OUT OF A TREE!"

"SKINDIVING?"

"I KNEW HE HAD TO BE GOOD
FOR SOMETHING."

"MANICURE."

"HAVE YOU SEEN A
LARGE, STRIPED TOM-CAT?"

"HOW'S GOOD OL' HEATHCLIFF?"

"A WORD WITH YOU..."

"BUZZ OFF!"

"I PUT A BELL ON HEATHCLIFF TO KEEP HIM
FROM SNEAKING UP ON BIRDS!"

"SMILE."

CLICK

"WHAT'S WRONG WITH OL' SMOKEY?"

"I WISH YOU WOULDN'T DO THAT!"

"PLEASE HOLD THE ROMANCE UNTIL I'VE
FINISHED PUTTING YOU OUT!"

"WHY DOES HEATHCLIFF ALWAYS BRING THAT
STUPID SCRATCHING POST ?!"

"THANKS."

"I SEE BIG TROUBLE AHEAD FOR SOMEONE
CLOSE TO YOU... YOUR DOG!!"

"OH, COME NOW, ALICE...
IT WAS ONLY A MOVIE."

"HOW COME WE NEVER SEE ANY BIRDS IN OUR BIRDBATH?"

"HE DOESN'T TRUST YOUR SCALE."

"HELP!"

"QUIT RUBBING IT IN!"

"IT'S THE VERY LATEST THING... A MILK BED."

"HERE'S YOUR TROUBLE."

"THE EARLY BIRD CATCHES HEATHCLIFF!"

"GET OUT THERE AND CHASE THAT CAT OUT OF OUR YARD!"

"*THAT* IS AGAINST THE RULES!"

"YOUR HANDKERCHIEF?... I THINK HEATHCLIFF HAS IT."

"FOR HIS NEXT DEATH DEFYING FEAT,
THE GREAT BOLDINI WILL..."

"I WAS EXPECTING A BLONDE!"

"IN THIS HOUSE, EVEN AN *ANT* DOESN'T STAND A CHANCE OF SURVIVAL!"

"HE'S GIVING US ANOTHER CHANCE."

"WE'VE GOTTA TEAR DOWN THAT BALCONY!"

"GRANDMA, HAVE YOU SEEN MY COMIC BOOK?"

"I SHOULD HAVE WARNED YOU, PROFESSOR...NEVER MENTION 'CAT GUT' IN FRONT OF HEATHCLIFF!"

"I'M AFRAID HE DOESN'T THINK MUCH OF HIS NEW BOWL!"

"SO FAR, ALL WE'RE GETTING IS CANS OF CAT FOOD!"

© 1974
McNaught Synd., Inc.
11-12

"I BOUGHT FRESH SALMON, ANCHOVIES, SHRIMP SALAD, CHICKEN LIVERS, MARINATED HERRING, A CAN OF CAVIAR...

...AND A HALF A POUND OF BALONEY FOR YOU, DEAR."

11-14 © 1974 McNaught Synd., Inc.

"YOU DON'T HAVE TO GET ME EVERY LAST LEAF!"

"TONIGHT, HE'S CONDUCTING A ROCK FESTIVAL!"

"STAY UNDER YOUR BLANKET, DEAR... IT'S CHILLY."

"HMMM...DOES THAT SAY 8 QUARTS OR 3 QUARTS?
....WHERE ARE MY GLASSES?"

"I'D LIKE TO PURCHASE SOME NEW FENCING...
BUT HE HAS TO TRY IT OUT FIRST."

"TONIGHT, HE'S ON TAPE!"

"SOMEONE LEFT HIM A HUGE BLOCK OF STOCK."

"HE'S BEEN HERE BEFORE...YOU GIVE HIM HIS SHOT...
I'LL BE WAITING FOR YOU ON TOP OF THE FILE CABINET!"

© 1974
McNaught
Syndicate, Inc.

12-18

MERRY CHRISTMAS

"HEATHCLIFF!!"

1974 12-20
McNaught
Syndicate, Inc.

"A SET OF TRAINS, A BASKETBALL, A DUMP TRUCK..."

"BROOK TROUT, TUNA, RED SNAPPER, MACKEREL, CARP, STRIPED BASS, CODFISH, HERRING, FLOUNDER, PERCH..."

"COOL IT, HEATHCLIFF!...HERE COME TH' JUDGE!"

"I'LL PICK OUT THE TREE, IF YOU DON'T MIND!"

"GUESS WHO GOT INTO YOUR CHRISTMAS SPARKLES?"

"THEY JUST DON'T MAKE 'EM THE WAY THEY USED TO!"

FREE KITTENS

"HEATHCLIFF WANTS TO MAKE SURE THAT EACH
LITTLE ONE RECEIVES A CHRISTMAS PRESENT."

"HEATHCLIFF CERTAINLY ENJOYS THE CHRISTMAS TREE."

"MR. NUTMEG...HEATHCLIFF WAS IN HERE....
GUESS WHAT HE DID TO TODAY'S SPECIAL?!"

"MY!...HE CERTAINLY IS A GROUCHY
BABY PHOTOGRAPHER!"

"STOP THIEF!"

"OH, BROTHER!...THEY'LL BE SOME HOWLING
ON THE BACK FENCE TONIGHT!"

"ALL RIGHT, FANS...LET'S HAVE ANOTHER LOOK
AT THAT ON INSTANT REPLAY..."

"ANOTHER ONE ?!!"

"NO, I HAVEN'T SEEN YOUR LOST JUMPROPE...
BUT I'LL KEEP AN EYE OPEN FOR IT."

"SCAT!"

"...AND LEADING AS THEY HIT THE STRETCH, IT'S...IT'S..."

"IT WORKS LIKE A CHARM!...BUT I HAVE A LOT OF TROUBLE WITH CATS!"

"I FELT IT WAS ONLY FAIR TO TELL HIM HE'S ADOPTED."

"OKAY... NOW YOU HAVE **EIGHT** LIVES LEFT!"

"I WANT YOU TO QUIT GIVING THAT CONFOUNDED HEATHCLIFF RIDES IN YOUR DOLL CARRIAGE!"

"TONIGHT, HE'S DOING 'PAGLIACCI'!"

"HEATHCLIFF'S NOT TOO IMPRESSED WITH YOUR AIM!"

"TWO PIES TO GO... ONE WITH PEPPERONI
AND ONE WITH FISH HEADS."

"CUT THAT OUT!"

"TIME FOR DIN-DIN, BABY."

"GO FOR HELP, DUMMY!"

"HE'S VERY FOND OF DA VINCI."

"CANCEL THOSE FROG'S LEGS!"

"HEATHCLIFF GOT A SPECIAL AWARD...
'BEST ALLEYCAT IN SHOW'."

2-25

"OH, YOU MIGHT BE ABLE TO
SHAKE HIM OUT OF A TREE...

...BUT HE ALWAYS LANDS
ON HIS FEET."

"YOU'LL HAVE TO POSTPONE THE CONCERT
UNTIL YOUR STAGE DRIES."

"I KNOW *YOU* CAN TOUCH YOUR TOES!!"

"SORRY, NO HITCH-HIKERS!!"

"THREE PEOPLE RESIDE HERE...ALTHOUGH
SOMETIMES IT SEEMS LIKE FOUR."

"LUGWRENCH..."

"FASTER, CLANCY! FASTER!!"

"TOO LATE."

"I THINK HE'S SUING YOU FOR MALPRACTICE!"

"I JUST KNOW HE'S GOING TO MAKE ME BREAK A BOTTLE!...HE'S PERFORMING HIS 'MILK DANCE'!"

"IT'S 'SARAH'S SWEET SHOP'!...SOMETHING ABOUT
HEATHCLIFF RIFLING EASTER BASKETS!'"

"SPRING IS SPRUNG!...THE GRASS IS RIS!..."

I WONDER WHERE
THE BIRDIES IS ?!

WHAT IS THE BEST GIFT YOU CAN EVER GIVE A HEATHCLIFF FAN OR ANY CAT FANCIER?

A YEAR'S SUBSCRIPTION TO THE HEATHCLIFF ASSOCIATION, OF COURSE!

This Association is not a toy or a nonbeneficial club. It's an organization with clear meaningful purposes. In fact, 10% of the yearly membership dues will be donated to recognized animal shelters and research organizations. The initial Association kit will include an organizational folder for your quarterly newsletters, a membership certificate (suitable for framing) and a special surprise Heathcliff souvenir. The newsletters will be informative on feline care, advancements made in disease research, upcoming events, new products, interesting feline stories, breeding news and, of course, some Heathcliff humor by George Gately. Many other noteworthy and fun topics will be covered, including a classified section.

YEARLY MEMBERSHIP DUES $12.00

NAME *(Please   print)*   *ADDRESS*

_____   _____

_____   _____

_____   _____

_____   _____

I've enclosed my check or money order in the amount of $_____ payable to Licensed Ventures International, Ltd., 300 East 42nd Street, New York, N.Y. 10017